L. A. Czarnecki

The Hero of Italy and other Poems

L. A. Czarnecki

The Hero of Italy and other Poems

ISBN/EAN: 9783741144226

Manufactured in Europe, USA, Canada, Australia, Japa

Cover: Foto ©Andreas Hilbeck / pixelio.de

Manufactured and distributed by brebook publishing software (www.brebook.com)

L. A. Czarnecki

The Hero of Italy and other Poems

THE HERO OF ITALY

AND

OTHER POEMS.

BY

MRS L. A. CZARNECKI,

AUTHORESS OF GENERAL BEM AND OTHER POEMS,
&c., &c.

EDINBURGH:
PATON & RITCHIE.

1861.

THE AUTHORESS

DEDICATES THIS WORK MOST RESPECTFULLY

(BY PERMISSION,)

TO HIS EXCELLENCY THE RIGHT HONOURABLE

THE EARL OF CARLISLE,

LORD LIEUTENANT OF IRELAND,

AS A SMALL TRIBUTE OF RESPECT

FOR

THE HIGH LITERARY ATTAINMENTS

WHICH HAVE EVER DISTINGUISHED HIS CAREER,

AS WELL AS FOR

THE WORTH OF HIS PUBLIC AND PRIVATE CHARACTER,

WHICH HAS GAINED FOR HIM UNIVERSAL ESTEEM.

CONTENTS.

	PAGE.
THE HERO OF ITALY,	1
THE HERO OF ITALY, IN MARCH 1861,	8
THE HEATHER HILLS OF SCOTLAND,	10
THE SHIPWRECK,	14
THOUGHTS ON FRANCIS II. BEFORE HIS FLIGHT FROM NAPLES,	20
A SUMMER MORNING,	23
WAR AND PEACE,	25
YOUTHFUL DAYS,	27
THE TWO PATHS,	29
THE HAWTHORN TREE,	31
THE RISING DAY,	33
HOPE,	35
SIR THORALD,	39
CHRISTIAN LOVE,	45
THE TOLLING OF THE BELL,	49
FAITH,	51
VICTORIA,	54
HYMN FOR 1861,	55
HUMAN STARS,	57
THE PAST,	61
REVENGE,	65
PETERBOROUGH CATHEDRAL,	67
TO JAMES Y. SIMPSON, ESQ., M.D., &C., &C.,	71
POLAND SHALL EXIST AGAIN,	73
A HUNTING SONG,	75
ON SEEING A BROKEN FONT LYING ON THE GROUND NEAR THE RUINS OF AN ANCIENT CHAPEL,	77
VERSES TO A RIVER,	78

CONTENTS.

	PAGE.
THE BEREAVED MOTHER,	79
THE SUMMER DAY IS DONE,	83
TO DIAMOND, A PET CANARY,	84
KIND WORDS,	85
ON A FAVOURITE DOG,	88
THOU SHALT BE LOVED BY ME,	90
THE PRAIRIE OF THE FAR WEST,	91
SEPTEMBER,	95
TO A BEAUTIFUL SLEEPING CHILD,	96
VERSES TO A LADY,	97
HEALTH,	99
ON A BUNCH OF WITHERED FLOWERS,	100
ON VIEWING A RUINED CASTLE BY MOONLIGHT,	102
WATER,	104
TRUE HAPPINESS,	109
A TRAVELLER VIEWING THE GREAT PRAIRIE FOR THE FIRST TIME,	115
VERSES TO A * * *,	119
THOUGHTS ON THE DEATH OF A TYRANT,	121

THE HERO OF ITALY.

SEA SHORE OF CAPRERA.

(Written December, 1860.)

Thou surging mighty sea,
  Thy billows loud did roar;
And nought was heard but thee,
  Upon that lonely shore.

The air was wrapt in gloom,
  And silent as the graves,
Except the swelling boom,
  And thunder of thy waves.

Fit time and scene to feel,
  To fire and rouse the heart;
To plan a country's weal—
  Struck down by slavery's dart.

To nerve the soul alone,
  For daring bold design;
Destroy a tyrant's throne,
  Or life itself resign.

Those generous thoughts revolved,
In the fearless soul of one
Who trod that shore, resolved
  On deeds to be dared and done.

Garibaldi! hero! victor!
  Thou whose bravest deeds are sung,—
Thou who art Italia's saviour,—
  Thou the theme of every tongue.

Thou dazzling soldier of renown;
  Who set Palermo proudly free,
Made tyranny no longer known,
  Along the shores of Sicily.

Who with a dauntless arm
    Freed the fairest gem of earth,
Naples! queen of every charm
    Owes to thee a second birth.

And the suffering patriot band,
    Who had bid the world farewell;
Freedom there at thy command,
    Lighted up their dungeon cell.

Struck the fetters from their hand—
    Unrivetted the galling chain,—
In the fight to proudly stand,
    True and willing men again.

And the haughty despot king,
    Had craven like to flee;
In his ears the cry did ring,
    Naples now is free!

No longer shall the tyrant
    Snake like erect his head ;
Or rule with looks defiant,—
    His power is as the dead.

No more shall the spoiler,
    Make a nation weep,—
The cruel fell destroyer,
    Does a bitter harvest reap.

He, who God's fair works defaced,
    To gratify his hate,
Is now a spectacle disgraced—
    A well deserved fate.

Victorious warrior, thou did stand
    In that triumphant hour ;
Round thee thy devoted band,
    Did blessings on thee shower.

THE HERO OF ITALY.

A nation's thanks were thine—
  A kingdom at thy feet:
Bending low at thy shrine,
  Were the noble and the great.

True to thyself and honour's laws;
  No selfishness in thee;
Reward enough thy country's cause,
  That Italy may be free.

Though the deafening shouts ran high,
  That made the welkin ring;
Thou the first to raise the cry,
  That hailed Emmanuel Italy's king.

He the rich reward who got,—
  Did well deserve the same;
History cannot find a blot,
  Upon his honoured name.

THE HERO OF ITALY.

Chivalrous monarch, thou hast fought,
   In many a well won field,—
Ever, ever hast thou sought,
   Thy people's right to shield.

None worthier ever wore the crown,
   A kingdom gave to thee:
Tyranny thou hast trampled down.—
   Brave king of Italy.

*   *   *   *

Now back to Caprera's shore,
   The warrior chief has come,—
Back to the billowing roar,
   Of his sea-girt island home.

He waits the strife to be,
   His brave again to lead;
When Venice city of the sea,
   Shall proudly raise her head.

Garibaldi! now we leave thee,
  And in the coming fight,
May a mighty hand go with thee,—
  And God defend the right.

THE HERO OF ITALY, IN MARCH 1861.

GREAT chief! thy voice again is heard,
  Calling to thy brave band,
Again to unsheath their swords,
  Again for freedom stand.

On the banks of the rolling Tiber,
  Shall joyous shouts yet ring;
The proud Roman and the Lombard,
  Shall triumphal pæans sing.

Again shall the victor's crown
  Shine on thy noble brow;
A people's voice again be heard,
  Tyrannic power laid low.

THE HERO OF ITALY.

Fair Venice, lovely city,
　Shall like a queen arise;
Her sons shall freedom breathe,
　Pure as their native skies.

THE HEATHER HILLS OF SCOTLAND.

The traveller from dear Scotia's land,
    May have stood in Asian bowers ;
And inhaled the rich perfume,
    Wafted from Eastern flowers.

The Chinar and the Oleander,
    Those glories of the East,
Upon whose varied tinted bloom,
    His admiring eyes did feast.

And the graceful Almond tree,
    With budding blossoms drest,
Under whose pure and odorous branch,
    He found refreshing rest.

THE HEATHER HILLS OF SCOTLAND.

He may have sat on Judah's hills,
    Under the Palm tree's shade,
Or cooled himself 'neath the Olive boughs,
    When sleep his eyelids weighed.

Or when exploring Egypt's land,
    Scanning many an ancient pile,
He gathered the lovely Lotus flowers,
    By the waters of the Nile.

He may have traversed India's clime,
    Sat under the Banyan tree,
Whose broad leaves spreading far and wide,
    A wonderous sight to see.

He may have wandered o'er the plains
    Of the prairie, far, far west,
And gazed on the gorgeous virgin flowers,
    By human hand unpressed.

His soul may have drunk in the beauty
    He saw depicted there;
Rich flowers of every varied tint,
    In wild luxuriance rare.

But the heather flower of his native land,
    Is to him a sight more dear,
For it recalls his own loved home,
    Which he thinks of with a tear.

For tho' it cannot boast of beauty,
    And blossoms in the wild,—
Ah! it is dear to the exiled heart,
    Of Scotia's mountain child.

He thinks, when he sees thy purple bloom,
    How oft' he greeted thee
When pursuing the stately deer,
    Or ranging the mountain's free.

THE HEATHER HILLS OF SCOTLAND.

The heather hills of Scotia's land,
    To her children they are dear,
For they breathe of freedom dearly prized,
    By the heart of the mountaineer.

Sweet flower of the lonely moor,
    Thou art the joy and pride
Of every loyal Scottish heart;—
    Gem of the mountain side.

THE SHIPWRECK.

"Twas a rugged, bleak and barren shore,
No sound but eagle's cry, or ocean's roar,
The wild waves for ever beat and dashed
Like an avenging spirit to fury lashed ;
The bold o'erhanging cliffs like some grim giant
Scowled on that angry sea, with looks defiant
Huge black rocks as colossal phantoms stood,
And o'er them ever foamed the seething flood ;
The dark steep heights were dreary, waste and
    bare,
No blooming plant could find a nurture there :
The stern and barren savage wilds around
Shadowed the scene with grandeur most pro-
    found. -
No gentle wind ever kissed that faithless deep,

THE SHIPWRECK. 15

The strong wind of the north did o'er it sweep,
With furious power and blasting icy breath ;
Carrying in its train ruin and death.
The mariner ever feared that dangerous coast :
In those dark waters stately ships were lost :
Nature in wild, terrific sublimity reigned here,
Calling forth men's adoration and their fear.

* * * *

'Twas night, and such a thrilling scene,
Even that drear coast had never seen ;
The whirlwind rose in its awful power,
The rocks shook with the thunder's roar,
The lightning flashed with a fearful glare,
As if the angry waters it would dare.
The tortured ocean rushed in madness on,
The very cliffs were with it overflown,
Black drops of rain in heavy torrents fell,
And the boom of the tempest did roll and swell ;
The sight of the destroying vengeful waves,
Looked like so many yawning graves.

* * * *

THE SHIPWRECK.

Hark! what sound is that comes on the gale,
So like the sound of fear and human wail!
There! there again! surely it cannot be
That human souls are on that remorseless sea:
The fishermen from the hamlets hear it too—
Rush to the beach to see what they can do.
Alas! their fears are true, they did too surely
    guess,
It was a noble vessel in deep and dire distress.
The darkness of the night was such they could
    not see,
They only heard sharp cries of misery.
Blazing lights they placed on every height,
Hoping that would cheer them in their strait;
They could do nothing more, help they could
    not give,
For in that heavy surf no boat could live.

Alas! that stately ship was staggering to and
    fro,
With seven feet of water in her hold below;

THE SHIPWRECK.

Three hundred souls in pent and deep emotion,
Shuddered as they gazed on that tempestuous
  ocean.
'Twas pitiful the looks of that devoted crew
Who had abandoned hope, for well they knew
That the ship's hard sides, o'er which many
  seas did roll,
Would strike upon the rocks, or float off the
  shoal.
No pen can picture those faces of dismay—
None knew who'd live to see the coming day.
Through her rigging howling came the gale,
The efforts of the weary men of no avail:
Her anchor parted, hope was all in vain,
For like a rotten branch her cable snapped in
  twain.
The ship is sinking! was the frenzied cry
Of those who saw they must prepare to die.
Oh! the agony, language cannot tell—
When rose the piercing cry of a last farewell,—
Children shrieking in their wretched mother's
  clasp,—

Women clinging to their husbands with a maddening grasp,—
And brave men with despair in every glance,—
Others with their senses locked as in a trance:
All calling to their God, for Him to hear;
To their wild prayers He turned a deaf ear.
In that fearful moment loud shrieks rent the air:
The ship with two heavy lurches sunk for ever there!
Oh! how many clung to the quivering mast,
But soon swept off by the relentless blast.
As the waves dashed at the sinking deck,
Many a soul was washed from the wreck.
Some wildly fixed their straining eye
On the beacon lights, and on the sky,
To see if a shadow of hope was there—
No help, and they sunk with shrieks of despair:
Others when their last farewell was given
Sunk calmly down with a prayer to heaven.
Some sunk with a bitter thrilling cry,
For they felt it was dreadful for them to die.

THE SHIPWRECK.

Ah! fearful 'twas to see the struggles for life,
As they gasped in the fierce unequal strife,—
The waves with foaming heads upreared,
And with them numbers disappeared.
On, on they rolled with one fell sweep,
And down all sunk to the gaping deep!
Only two,—two exhausted men were saved
To tell the tale that on their hearts was 'grav'd.

THOUGHTS ON FRANCIS II.,

BEFORE HIS FLIGHT FROM NAPLES.

ALL-POWERFUL and Omniscient God!
  Who hearest every sigh,—
And from Thy heavenly throne,
  Looks down with watchful eye,—
Thou seest a fierce and mighty strife,
  Against a cruel tyrant foe,
Who would enslave the souls of men,
  And plunge their homes in woe.

THOUGHTS ON FRANCIS II.

Shall the Bourbon trample
    Rights human and divine;
Shall he deface the glorious earth,
    And barter what is Thine,—
Shall he exult and proudly boast,
    O'er the defenceless weak;
And on the brave and noble,
    His bitter malice wreak.

Has the blood of martyred thousands,
    All been shed in vain;
Shall the host of suffering captives,
    Still bear their load of pain.
And the tears of anguish shed,
    For Italy's drooping land;
While her exiled sons live pining
    On many a foreign strand.

Thou art the God of battles;
   The strength of hills is thine;
And thy almighty voice has said,
   Vengeance it is mine.
Thy sword thou wilt gird on,
   Thou will defend the right;
And a grim oppressive rule,
   Shall fall before thy sight.

Thou wilt arrest the spoiler,
   In his most triumphant hour;
Sweep him from his high estate,
   Destroy his fearful power.
Thou wilt be with the brave,
   Who march to meet the foe;
And go before them in the fight,
   And save a world from woe.

A SUMMER MORNING.

The morning comes, and the balmy breeze,
Is wafted from rich and leafy trees;
The lark's first hymn is heard aloft—
And the linnet's song so sweetly soft.
The blackbird's note is sounding high,
As if with a loud and joyous cry;
New beauty in every fragrant shade,
And verdure on every dewy glade.
And brighter the tint of every flower,
Refreshed by the cool of the morning hour;
While the waves of the glittering swelling sea,
Roll on to the shore right merrily.
Earth smiles with a radiant rosy glow,
Which the sultry day can never shew;
All nature is lovely, fresh, and fair,
And gemmed with beauty rich and rare.

A sight like this fills the mind with bliss,
And the heart is surcharged with happiness;
The eye that was heavy with sleepless night,
Beams afresh in the morning light.
The spirit feels light and gladly gay,
For earth and sky sheds a genial ray;
They fill the heart with love and gladness,
And chase away every thought of sadness,
For it rules with a sweetly soothing power,
The reign of the summer morning hour.

WAR AND PEACE.

The noble city dismantled and torn—
Of all its glory ruthlessly shorn,—
On the trampled field lie the ghastly dead,—
Victor and vanquished on a gory bed.
Fearful to gaze on their gaping wounds—
While the cannon's roar on the air resounds:
Sad scenes of violence on every road,
Wherever the usurping foe has trod.
Fond mothers wailing day and night,
For the loved ones fallen in the fight,—
Famine stalking with visage gaunt,
And helpless children dying for want.
Men's very nature is changed to hate,
Nought but revenge will their anger sate,—
Unheeded are the dearer ties of life,
Each goads another to the murderous strife;
Crushed to earth are all glorious things,
By the blighting havoc that war ever brings.

Radiant in beauty shone the day—
The sun o'er the hills shed his brilliant ray;
On the warm air came a rich perfume,
The trees hung thick with verdant bloom.
Pure and bright was the crystal rills,
And matchless in grandeur the sunny hills,
While the Sabbath bells pealed sweetly clear—
To the good and true so sacred and dear.
The old and the young hastened along,
To worship, and join in sacred song
Of praise to Him whose gracious power
Lights up every heavy and darksome hour;
And happy children sweet and fair,
Bent their steps to the house of prayer,—
'Twas a lovely scene worth gazing on,
For peace in rare perfection shone.

YOUTHFUL DAYS.

Who can forget their native home,
   Where'er their lot be cast;
Or the lightsome happy days,
   Where their youth was passed.

How carelessly they roved
   Among the blue wild flowers,—
How merrily they talked
   In those sunny hours—

Or climbed the beech trees boughs,
   Where the linnet sung—
Or merrily merrily roved,
   The forest trees among.

YOUTHFUL DAYS.

The loud and hearty laugh—
　　The joyous dance and song,
When forest flowers were wreathed
　　To deck the youthful throng.

Those young and smiling days,
　　They never come again,—
The sallies of artless mirth,
　　That did the heart enchain.

But sweet to memory yet,
　　Though the heart be dull with care
To think upon those days,
　　When all was pure and fair.

THE TWO PATHS.

Let not the little things of earth,
  Obtain a power o'er thee;
They cannot meet the soul's desires,
  For vain and false they be.

Lift up thy heavy laden eyes,
  And look another way,—
A path that leads to life and light,
  And things of brighter ray.

What though the road thou dost behold,
  A steep and strait one be,
Remember it will guide thee on
  Where the spirit shall be free.

Men for the world's fleeting wealth,
　　Will risk immortal life;
And in their thirsty love of gold,
　　Rush into sinful strife.

Destruction's path is broad and wide,—
　　There streams of pleasure flow;
But it only leads the weary feet,
　　To pains and endless woe.

The narrow path, tho' hard to tread,
　　A blessed one it is;
It leads thee where thy soul shall live
　　In sure and endless bliss.

THE HAWTHORN TREE.

The stately oak in the mossy wood,
   Stands like a king so proudly free ;
But I love better the fragrant shade,
   The pure white bloom of the hawthorn tree.

How oft have I stood at evening hour,
   Beneath the foliage of thy shade,
Gazed on the moonbeams calm and still
   Gild with beauty each hill and glade.

What so sweet as a cottage home,
   Thy white blossoms round it wreathed,
And tones of love from truthful lips,
   Under thy branches sweetly breathed.

THE HAWTHORN TREE.

Of all the radiant flowers that grow,
 None so sweet and pure to me,
As the lovely sight of the simple flower,
 That blooms upon the hawthorn tree.

THE RISING DAY.

Wake up, wake up, the stars of night
   Long since have sped their way;
And in their place the sun so bright
   Gilds new the rising day.
On every bush and shady tree,
   A feathery band unite;
In thrilling notes of triumph free,
   To welcome back the light.

Wake up, wake up, the blooming flowers
   Perfume the balmy air,
And in the green and shady bowers,
   Is fragrance rich and rare.

THE RISING DAY.

The lowing cattle, sounding sweet
   Down in the distant vale;
All living things now rise to greet,
   And give their Maker hail!

Wake! throw off the earthly load,
   And hymn a holy song,
To nature's universal God,—
   Blessings to Him belong.
Each little bird sings loud and clear,
   And heaven's vault is ringing;
Then up, and be thou without fear,
   Thy Maker's praises singing.

HOPE.

The human mind is formed for hope. In youth how fantastic are the visions that allure us, no sooner is one hope destroyed, than another is formed. It is part of the nature of man, ever to be hoping, ever to be conjuring up visions of rank, power, or wealth.

The warrior on the battlefield rushes into the thickest of the contest, dealing death at every step, hoping by his mighty deeds of arms to free his country from the enemy, and deck his brow with the laurels of victory,—that his name may have a place in the annals of history, and in the hearts of his admiring countrymen,—and that the name of hero may inscribed on his tomb.

The statesman exhausts his powers of diplomacy, and his voice of eloquence, he sacrifices health at the shrine of ambition, that a nation's worship, and a perishable immortality may be his.

The merchant embarks all that he possesses, he trusts it to the dangers of the deep, hoping that the return will bring him boundless wealth, and raise him above his fellows.

The sea beaten mariner hopes for sight of land, that he may behold those he loves, and spend his life with them.

The scholar trims the midnight lamp, withers the blood in his veins, deprives himself of rest, that the adulation and admiration of men may follow him, as the accomplished poet or profound historian.

All, then, from the highest to the lowest have their hopes, and all hope to have those hopes realized; but Ah! too often they elude their grasp, and the labours of a life-time perish in a moment. How widely different are they who live only in the hope of a blessed immortality, whose hope is sustained by faith in a redeeming and merciful Saviour; hope that is no delusion, but sure and stedfast, for it is a hope built upon the promises of Christ, that in six troubles He will be with them, and in the seventh He will not be far from them; He will put their enemies to shame, and raise them up from the very depths of affliction, — overcome all their difficulties, — make joyful the hour of death,—smooth the passage to the grave, and welcome to the kingdom of His Father.

But they who fly after the things of this world—who build their hopes on it—misfortune shall come upon them like an armed man, when they least expect it,—they shall cry to God in their trouble, but He will shut his ears to their call, and laugh when their fear cometh.

SIR THORALD.

The house stood on a lonely road,
Where footsteps of men seldom trod;
An ancient wall defended one side,
And the other was washed by ocean's tide.
An alley of thickly shaded trees,
That never was stirred by summer breeze,
Enveloped it round with a sable gloom,
Like the darkness of the silent tomb.
In that dark wood no plaintive dove
Ever sang his melting lay of love;
No little bird in the morning ray,
Ever trilled his happy gladsome lay.
No music, but the solemn sounding sea,
With its wild deep thrilling melody;
No flowers bloomed, they sunk in decay,
For the dark trees shut out the sunny day.

The very air around that gloomy spot
Seemed fraught with anxious care and thought;
Fit place for one whom crushing woe
Had laid every young and bright hope low:
Sir Thorald had won for himself a name
In the ranks of death's undying fame;
Ever brave and fearless in the fight,
He dared the boldest deeds of might.
He had stood in the breach when few were near,
Without one pang or look of fear,—
His valour was the burden of many a song—
His name the theme of every tongue.
With joy he thought of the time to come,
When he would speed to his dear loved home,
See her who held his heart in thrall—
The dearly loved, the prized of all.
Her smiles that would dearly him repay,
For all he had borne in the battle's fray;
The music of her sweet and silvery tone,
His only beloved and worshipped one.
He came, and what a sad tale was told

To him who had hastened his bride to behold,—
He listened till his face wore the hues of death—
He heard she had broke every vow of faith.
The friend of his youth, who shared every
  thought,
Was he who basely this treachery wrought.
Yes! the one he had loved with faithful heart,
Had acted this cruel and shameful part;
Wrung a proud and noble soul with pain,
And closed his heart to hope again.
He sought not again warlike strife,
But lived a moody despairing life
In that old house by the sounding sea,
And the wild waves his only company.
His heart grew chill through a life so lone,
His generous thoughts and deeds seemed gone;
Doubts of all good shadowed his breast—
His bitter feelings gave him no rest,
Such was the dreadful state of mind
Which deceit had wrought in that nature kind.
For years he existed in sadness alone,

Neither pride nor passion on his visage shone,—
What a life for one, who had bravely stood,
And shed his blood for his country's good.

* * * *

'Twas a hot and silent summer night,
No moon beamed with a softened light;
The brooks with drought, were hard and dry,
And the sea birds uttered their piercing cry.
Ocean moaned as if it could not rest,
As if in pain that would not be suppressed—
A fearful darkness curtained round the air—
No familiar face could be discerned there:
Sir Thorald on that dark mysterious night,
Stood on a lonely mountain height;
Nought was heard but the heaving of the ocean—
His heart beat with strange and wild emotion.
He felt oppressed as if he could not breathe,
As if he felt the icy hand of death—
As if some master hand decreed his fate,—
He could not think, he felt so desolate,
He gazed up to the sky, if he could trace

One speck of light in all the boundless space.
Thick darkness it was there and everywhere.
The first time in many years he breathed a
 prayer.
He felt as if he was in the land of dreams,
Where all was shade, no sunny beams,
Of gladsome light on him to pour,—
He thought to earth he would return no more:
He looked despairing upward, yet again
His bounding heart beat high, but not with pain,
For lo! he saw the heavens cleft open there,
And out there flew an angel messenger,—
Floods of radiant light encompassed him around,
And on the air there came a murmuring sound,—
As he downward flew there was clearly seen
In his angel hand a branch of gorgeous green,
Thick with buds and leaves, breathing a perfume
Of heavenly beauty and immortal bloom.
Straight he came to him whose heart was swell-
 ing
With fierce emotion, past all language telling,—

Thorald! the angel said, thy Father sends thee
  this,
This budding branch, to thee it will bring bliss;
Put it in thy bosom, for with thee it must
  bloom,—
It will chase away thy sadness and thy gloom.
Thou hast forgot thy Maker, he remembered thee,
Retrieve the past, employ thy talents worthily;
Let faith be thy assurance, suffer and endure,
Good works thy atonement, thy recompense
  shall be sure,—
Farewell, O Thorald! remember well this hour
When thy God preserved thee from an evil
  power.

* * * *

Sir Thorald's face was calm, it looked no longer
  blanched,
His warring soul and fierce emotion quenched.
No scowling look upon that noble face,—
In his soul no bitter feelings had a place.
His life was full of actions great and good,

He in the senate of his country stood;
Where with a voice of eloquent appeal,
He pleaded truly for his country's weal.
Wherever there was want, or fell despair,
He gave, and kindly soothed the brow of care;
For ever doing good,—now no wasted time,—
Goodness crowned his life, his noble deeds
    sublime.
He had no more that quick imperious tread,
Benevolence o'er his face was kindly spread;
In his halls a loving heart presided there,
And a group of little children sweet and fair;
Whose merry voices rang out loud and clear,
Resounding sweetly on the echoing air.
And often as the summer day grew dim,
Softly would they sing their evening hymn;
Sir Thorald loved to listen in that sweet hour,
For it spoke to his soul with soothing power.
Yes! the branch that had come from a heavenly
    land,
Had bloomed and rewarded his faithful hand.

CHRISTIAN LOVE.

WHAT a noble feeling in the heart is Christian Love. How it elevates in the scale of being those that possess it, — refines their mind, — throws the grace of beauty over all their actions,—surrounds them with a radiant halo of brightness, which worldly riches and grandeur fail to impart. Who can estimate its value, or set a price upon it? Not all the diamonds of Golconda could purchase it. It is a gift which only the Most High can give. When Porus, the Indian King, was asked by the Macedonian Hero, his conqueror, how he desired to be treated? "Like a king," was the reply; adding, "all things are included in that single word." So all that is lovely, all that is pure, noble, and good, is included in the single word

Love. It makes us feel the mighty obligations we lie under to our God,—the mighty debt we owe a Saviour, who died that we might be saved, and made fit for the kingdom of His Father. It covers us with the robe of humility. It is above every Christian grace. Our faith may be great, and our hopes of grace strong, but without Christian love we are nothing. It instils charity and forbearance into all our thoughts and actions. The heart under the influence of this most beautiful feeling swells forth spontaneous emotions of supplication, entreaty, and praise at the foot of the throne. And He whose power is illimitable, whose mercy is boundless, hears, and bestows upon them every good and perfect gift. Oh! thou whose heart is burdened, seek the way everlasting, pray that thy soul may experience the exceeding peace and joy that springs from Christian love. It will cause thee to love all mankind,—feel for and assist thy suffering brother,—view with charity their fail-

CHRISTIAN LOVE. 47

ings,—striving humbly to correct their vices,—shewing them the way to that goal which thou thyself art aiming at. Without such feelings none can stand before their Maker. Do all this, and exceeding great will be thy reward,—even the praise of Him whose praise is praise in very truth. His words to thee shall be well done good and faithful servant,—the crown of glory shall be placed upon thy brow, and the enjoyment of a blessed eternity be thine for ever.

> The gems that deck the kingly crown,
>   They shine not half so bright,
> As the true and loving heart,
>   In doing what is right.

> Lovely are the springing flowers,
>   In all their varied dyes,—
> Lovelier far the beams of love,
>   Which light up grateful eyes.

CHRISTIAN LOVE.

Noble is the victor's crown
The soldier strives to win;
Nobler yet the Christian love
That forgives another's sin.

THE TOLLING OF THE BELL.

THE few following lines were attempted after reading an account of the last moments of Rasella, the noble Italian Patriot, (who along with other devoted men had been confined in prison for many years.) When he heard the tolling of the bell that announced that the hour of his execution had arrived, he exclaimed "Has it come at last, this hour so long prayed for! I am happy now!" When Rasella arrived at the place of execution, all his companions in captivity were decapitated before his eyes, for the purpose of intimidating him,—he was asked if he would recant his opinions,—he replied, "Never." Another question was put to him, if he would receive absolution,—he rejected it. A priest then stepped forward, holding in his hand a crucifix, upon which was a figure of the Redeemer, and said, "Surely he would at least kiss that," "Ah! willingly will I do that!" exclaimed Rasella. As he kissed it, he uttered these significant words, "Yes, He too was a liberal."

HARK! I hear the bell—

Life's pilgrimage is nearly o'er,—

My spirit soon shall wing,

To that far viewless shore.

Soon shall I cross that bourne,
   Never, never to return,—
My heart is now at peace,
   Who then for me would mourn!

Farewell, ye prison walls,
   I now no longer sigh,
My earthly cares are past,
   My greatest bliss to die.

At length, at length it comes,
   This hour so long delayed,—
For which my weary, weary soul
   For years has often prayed.

Oh! God and Heavenly Father,
   Uphold and strengthen me
Through this fearful scene of gore,
   That leads me up to Thee.

FAITH.

How replete with comfort and consolation is the possession of faith. What an ordeal of hopes and fears the Christian has to go through before his heart truly believes, with a stedfast and sure reliance upon the efficacy of divine love. The soul must be thoroughly weeded from the tares which have sprung up in it, and that threaten to destroy the good seed. No lurking doubt, no unholy thought must have place where all should be light. The temple must be purified, and the tempter driven from his stronghold, before a pure and holy faith can enter. Prayer is here all powerful,—We must pray, pray without ceasing—wrestle with God even as Jacob wrestled with the angel and prevailed,—our prayer must be the same as his,—" I will not let thee go till thou hast blessed me;" and the same God who blessed that patriarch of old, and who is the same yesterday, to day, and forever, He will bless thee, making His presence known through saving faith. Happy is the heart when that holy principle is bestowed upon it.—Wordly misfortunes become light, affliction is sanctified, calumny and persecutions meekly endured,—the sneers of the scoffer fall harmlessly, for it is protected by a shield and breastplate that the world cannot give, neither can it take away; even the shield of faith and breastplate of salvation. Rich are they who trust in their Maker, seeking nothing but to praise and honour Him. Ever striving to enter in at the strait gate,—ever watching, ready to meet the Lord at his coming. Ye who are distracted with the cares of this world—who seek peace and cannot find it—come to Him and He will sustain. He will not cast thee away,—thou art precious in His sight, sin-laden though thou art; cry to him from the depths of thy soul—yea, cry with an exceeding great voice,—like Esau, when he cried, " Bless me, even me also, O my father!" Be that thy prayer, and He will not desert thee at thy need,—He will give thee the love that purifieth—the hope that trusteth, and the faith that will bring thee to his throne.

> Faith frees the burdened soul,
>   For pure is its belief;
> It brightens every heavy thought,
>   Dismisses every grief.
>
> Without believing humble faith,
>   The crown we cannot gain;
> We cannot see God's face,
>   Until we faith attain.

VICTORIA.

Virtue encircles thee, beloved Queen!
Integrity and grace are around thee seen—
Calumny cannot cast upon thee a stain :
Thou hast striven true goodness to attain.
Oh, may the blessings of Almighty love
Rest ever on thee, from thy God above ;
In peace and safety may thou long reign,—
And after death heaven's crown obtain.

HYMN FOR 1861.

Dry up the tear of sadness,
   And loud hosannas sing;
With chastened voice of gladness,
   To heaven's almighty King.

For like a star in glory,
   Comes in another year;
Oh, let our hearts be holy,
   And filled with godly fear.

Let every thought and word,
   Deep gratitude convey
To a gracious sovereign Lord;
   Our only hope and stay.

HYMN FOR 1861.

May we in this new-born year,
  From all temptation flee;
Attend his voice and truly hear
  If we his face would see.

May they who sorrow's path have trod,
  Find this a happy year;
For in it they have found their God,
  And He his children dear.

Then dry the tear of sadness,
  And loud hosannas sing;
With chastened voice of gladness,
  To heaven's almighty King.

HUMAN STARS.

There is a soft and hallowed light,
   While life lasts never dies;
It is the pure and loving beam
   That shines from mothers' eyes:
They penetrate our wants,
   They soothe the greatest grief,
Diffusing with their potent spell,
   Sweet and sure relief.

There is another stronger light
   That guides the treacherous way,
Lending by its steady gleam
   A sure supporting stay:

HUMAN STARS.

It is the flash that lights
    A father's loving eye;
Who guides the stumbling youth
    With many a heaving sigh.

There is a mild and constant light
    Shining on many a path;
Healing many a household breach—
    And soothing words of wrath,—
It is the star that glows
    From sisters' loving eyes;
Before whose pure and virtuous glance,
    Guilt takes wings and flies.

There is a brighter, bolder light,
    Shedding a radiant cheer,
On many a young unhappy breast,
    Depressed by needless fear,—

HUMAN STARS.

It is the proud and honest look,
   In a brother's eye that lives,—
When with a strong and willing arm
   He firm protection gives.

There is a sure and steady light,
   Blessings from it flow;
Throwing a lustre o'er life's path,
   Soothing many a woe.
It is the fervent noble gaze,
   Welling from true friends' eyes,—
A light that ever, ever shines,
   And never, never dies.

Those brilliant stars they gild—
   They gem the weary way,
They are the joy, the hope—
   The solace and the stay

HUMAN STARS.

Of many a gay or thoughtful heart,
Who love such lights to shine,—
And few there be who do not need
Those human stars divine.

THE PAST.

The past, the strange and dreamy past,
    It often fills the heart with pain;
Feelings we thought slumbered deep,
    Burst from the soul relief to gain.

Some think of the happy days long fled,
    Years of joy which have o'er them flown,—
Of early recollections fondly loved,
    In the abyss of time for ever gone.

For treasured deep in memory's halls,
    Is the thought of the loved and dear,—
The eyes that ever beamed with truth,
    And the voice which charmed the ear.

And every spot or flowery path
   Where happy hours have fled;
They only give now quivering pain
   For they recall the beloved dead.

Others mourn great hopes laid low,
   When their pride, the young and brave,
In the midst of victorious battle won,
   Fought, and found an early grave.

Or clouds have darkened the sunny day,
   When woe has the mind dismayed;
Or the trusting heart wrung with pain,
   When by foul treachery betrayed.

Others weep for their early dead,
   Lying low in the ocean deep;
Storms above their heads sound high,
   And wind and waves their revel keep.

THE PAST.

And some recall days of gloom,
   When their heart breathed many a sigh;
When nights were spent in deep despair,
   And silent waking agony.

When no human voice spoke of hope,
   And their home was dull and lone;
They seemed by all of earth forgot,
   For their glory it was gone.

Others again think of the past,
   As they would of a tale sublime;
No rending grief had pained their life,
   In that happy good old time.

For hope and the voice of love,
   Had crowned their noble life;
To them the past was a pleasant dream,
   With no worn out spirit's strife.

THE PAST.

The past, the dreamy silent past,
   It has a strong undying power;
Weaves such various trains of thought,
   In memory's deep and silent hour.

In busy scenes of life we may forget—
   The spell of feeling cannot last;
But still the mystic hour will come,
   Tears will fall thinking of the past.

REVENGE.

Like to a fierce and raging fire,
Consuming with uncontrolled desire,—
Like the hawk, who robs the poor bird's nest,
To tear in pieces the fluttering breast,—
Like the subtle serpent who pants to spring,
And give to the helpless the deadly sting,—
Like the ruthless tiger, tho' gorged with food,
Still waits and watches and scents for blood,—
Like the cruel vulture, keen and grey,
Viewing ravenously his destined prey;
Such are they who wrong to avenge,
Burn with wild unhallowed revenge.
They rob their life of every earthly joy—
Give to themselves a dreadful destiny,—
Their heart is torn with passion strong,
As they think of their real or fancied wrong.

F.

They have no grace nor trusting faith,
They live, but it is a living death,
Their heart is seared in its deepest core,
And their eyes are lit with a sullen lour;
Their days are spent in fitful gloom,
They blight all hope and youthful bloom,
They gloat o'er the time when they shall avenge,
And exult o'er the victim of their revenge.

* * * *

Such who keep vengeance in their heart,
They cannot hope to have a part
With Him whose life was one of love—
Gentle and kind as the meek-eyed dove.
They will never behold that seraphic face,
Nor live in the beauty of that holy place.
If feelings of such a deadly stain
Live in their heart, hope is vain;
Whatever their talent, rank, or station,
They are vile weeds in God's creation:
For "I, the Almighty, I will avenge,"
Are words of Him who hates men's revenge.

PETERBOROUGH CATHEDRAL

Is one of the finest relics of ecclesiastical architecture that England possesses. To walk through the magnificent aisles of the Cathedral, and look around upon the rich and rare devices with which it is covered, the heart feels that it is indeed in a temple fit for the Almighty to be worshipped, and His praises to be sung.

The foundation stone of the first Monastery was laid in the year of our Lord 654, it was destroyed by fire in 1116. The foundation stone of the present building was laid in 1117, the transept completed in 1150. The nave and western gateway built, and the painted ceiling executed by Benedict in 1177 and 1199. The height of the painted ceiling is eighty one feet, the choir, seventy five feet,—from the altar table to the east window thirty eight feet, and from the west door to the east window four hundred and twenty two feet. The interior of the choir is rich in the highest degree. In the north aisle lies buried Catherine of Arragon, beneath a black marble slab. The daughter, the sister, the wife and mother of kings, after all her many sorrows, she sleeps well. Also in the north aisle is a very ancient shrine, supposed to be that of St Ibba; north of the apse is Bishop Gedda's monument,—the first Christian monument erected. The new building called Lady Chapel, and which is a superb addition to the Cathedral, was built by Abbots Kirton and Ashton from 1410 to 1500. The ceiling is perhaps the finest in existence.

PETERBOROUGH CATHEDRAL.

When we gaze upon this splendid structure, scan all its gorgeous beauties, its varied workmanship, its ancient Chapels, and windows of strange fashion and value, the relics of other times with which it is filled, the heart feels when it looks on all this emotions of admiration and solemnity.

Gorgeous relic of the past,
   Thy beauty is sublime;
Standing as if for aye to last—
   Defying grim old time.

Every strange device within thee
   Tells of a bygone day;
Our thoughts when gazing on thee
   To other years do stray.

When the abbot and monks knelt round
   The sacred altar there;
And the organ pealed with mighty sound
   Through chapels rich and rare.

PETERBOROUGH CATHEDRAL.

The solemn swell of the mass rung high,
  And the sacred benediction given;
Then many hearts did breathe a sigh,
  And fix their thoughts on heaven.

Years are gone when the midnight chime
  Rung dolefully for the loss
Of those who fought in that olden time,
  Brave soldiers of the cross.

Yes, gone are the mighty days of old,
  When those ancient aisles of thine
Were filled with the lovely and the bold,
  To kneel at St Ibba's shrine.

Time does ever change, and they
  Who did before it bow,
Alas! they all have vanished away—
  Are dust and ashes now.

PETERBOROUGH CATHEDRAL.

The illustrious sons of earth,
　　Of high and honoured name,
Of princely title and noble birth,
　　And many a name of fame.

And England's sorrow-stricken queen,
　　At whose sad tale we weep,—
The good and royal Catherine,
　　In thy north aisle does sleep.

Those great and mighty dead,
　　They do sleep well with thee;
A hallowed glory is o'er them shed,
　　Forgot they ne'er shall be.

Though dead, their memory is not vain,
　　For thou dost proudly stand;
And may thou long with us remain,
　　To beautify our land.

To JAMES Y. SIMPSON, Esq., M.D.

(Professor in the University of Edinburgh.)

Son of genius, thou whose honoured name
Fills a noble rank upon the scroll of fame—
Whose works are known and valued far and wide,—
Great men of talent take thee as their guide.
Through the dark vista of a bygone day
Thy knowledge hewed a new and clearer way;
Many obstacles were cast down on that road,
But triumphant in wisdom onward thou trod;
Priceless was the boon thou didst bestow
On suffering mortals by agony laid low;
Pain, through thy research and potent will,
Succumbed, soothed by thy matchless skill.

TO JAMES Y. SIMPSON, ESQ., M.D.

Hero of science, just, great, and good,
Mankind owes thee a debt of gratitude.
Well may Scotia honour her illustrious son,
Who by might of intellect has such good deeds
    done.
Emblazoned on her brightest page of fame
Shall endure for ever Simpson's name.

POLAND SHALL EXIST AGAIN.

POLAND shall yet exist,—
    She shall be free again;
The blood she has poured forth
    Shall not be shed in vain.

Happy hearts shall again be seen
    Within her castle halls,—
Victory's flag shall gaily hang
    On Warsaw's ancient walls.

Kosciuszko's heart yet lives
    In the breast of many a Pole;
Their swords will flash with life,
    When war's deep thunders roll.

POLAND SHALL EXIST AGAIN.

Poland shall yet arise,
    And with her warrior band,
Sweep off the invading foe
    Who has usurped her land.

She is waiting for the hour,
    That like a trumpet blast
Shall come to wake the brave,
    And freedom gain at last.

Poland shall exist again,
    The laurel bind her brow,
And they who robbed her rights
    Low in the dust shall bow.

Note.—April, The scenes of bloodshed daily witnessed in the streets of Warsaw upon an oppressed people, have elicited the following generous sentiments from Garibaldi. The *Diritto* publishes a letter of the 14th, addressed by General Garibaldi to M. Hartzen, in London. Garibaldi says that the emancipation of the serfs in Russia has been hailed with gratitude in Europe, and has placed the Czar on a par with the most illustrious benefactors of the human race. That work of kindness has been now sullied by the blood of an innocent people, and it is the duty of all who have applauded the first measure to throw a curse on those who have been guilty of the latter.

A HUNTING SONG.

Up, up and away o'er moor and fell,
    The morning looks so gay,—
Up, up and away ye huntsmen bold,
    And bring the stag to bay.

The sun peeps out so clear and bright,
    The hounds are in full cry;
The gallant horse, as he leaps the fence,
    On the wings of the wind does fly.

The merry ho! ho! of the jovial band,
    Falls cherrily on the ear,—
The day puts on a laughing face,
    To greet such sounds of cheer.

A HUNTING SONG.

The joyous note of the hunting horn
   Is heard on the echoing hills ;
The hearty notes ring clear and high,—
   The air with music fills.

Up, up and away, o'er moor and fell,
   The morning looks so gay,—
Up, up and away ye huntsmen bold,
   And bring the stag to bay.

LINES

ON SEEING A BROKEN FONT LYING ON THE GROUND NEAR THE RUINS OF AN ANCIENT CHAPEL.

That shattered font does strangely tell
   A tale of other years,
When on the young head prayers flowed,
   With many hopes and fears.

They all have faded—gone,
   Swept off from mortal ken;
And trampling on thy poor remains,
   Are a race of other men.

VERSES TO A RIVER.

Rush on, thou mighty river,
    Rush on to the sounding sea;
Rush on in gladness ever,
    Deep music's heard in thee.

Rush on like a thunder-cloud,
    Defying all control,—
Like the blast of the trumpet loud,
    Stirring up the hero's soul.

Rush on like the tempest blast,
    Rush on, and be thou free,—
Rush, and joyfully gain at last
    Thy home in the boundless sea.

THE BEREAVED MOTHER.

She sits alone in her gloomy dwelling,
Her heart with grief for ever swelling;
Her face no hope of gladness wears,
For anguish at her bosom tears.
She thinks of the time when voices sweet,
With loving gladness aye did her greet,—
Of the prayers breathed at each little bed,
And blessings showered on the loved head,—
Of the youthful forms sweet and fair,—
Now all around is silent there.
She glances at the deserted room,
As if she thought they yet would come.
But no; the weary years go slowly on,
And still she mourns, that lonely one,
Husband and children, all have gone,
Leaving her desolate and alone.

THE BEREAVED MOTHER.

She sits heart-stricken, sorely grieved,
For of all her hopes she is bereaved.

  * * * *

The loved of her youth, pride of her heart,
Was the first from her loving arms to part;
On Inkerman's bloody field he fell—
His deeds his country's page will tell.
Ah! that poor wife, what tears she shed,
Thinking of that far off gory bed.
The eldest son, her stay and joy,
A noble, bold, and gallant boy,
Found a grave in the ocean deep,
Where winds and waves o'er him sweep.
Her second boy, good, young, and brave,
He too found an early grave,
The ardent sun of India's clime
Withered his youth in its sweetest prime;
He lies in a tomb of the desert sand,
Struck by the heat of that scorching land.
And another yet, her last and only one,
Her third, her fairest youngest son;

THE BEREAVED MOTHER.

He upon whose fearless loving face
The features of his father she could trace,
His was the sudden, saddest fate of all,
And fearfully on her the blow did fall.
One morn he went forth smiling, gay,
Ere night he was senseless mangled clay.
She could not speak, her heart seemed rent in
    twain,
All thought she ne'er could breathe again,
For her poor soul had so closely clung
To this her youngest, best, and only one :
Many months she quite unconscious lay,
Remembering nothing of that awful day,
In agonizing accents calling on his name,
And wondering why he never, never came.
Once more her aching head was free from pain,
And then returning reason came again ;
They told her gently of her last lost boy,—
She listened with paling lip and dimming eye,
She knew now she was reft and lone,
To her the smiles of earth were gone.

THE BEREAVED MOTHER.

Her heart was no more filled with wild despair,
Calm but silent sorrow shone out there.
She wandered always 'neath the old oak tree,
Where oft her children played in fancy free;
Or in the twilight lingered by his tomb,
Till night was heavy and dark with gloom;
Or sat at the casement, where in happy years,
She had gazed on her treasures with hopes and
 fears:
And had hailed with delight their joyous play,
When they shouted with glee in the garden
 gay,—
Or she sought in that best of books relief,
For comfort and strength to bear her grief;
Thus did her days wearily pass away,
And her sore tried soul did meekly pray,
That to her the boon would soon be given
To join her loved and lost in heaven.

THE SUMMER DAY IS DONE.

The summer day is done,
   All is hushed on hill and bower;
Birds to their nests have gone,
   'Tis the pleasant evening hour.

'Tis the hour for the musing mind
   To wing its flight from earth;
From the wreck of the past to find
   Pure hopes of brighter birth.

It sheds a soft and blissful calm
   Upon the throbbing breast;
Like a sweet and healing balm,
   Gently lulling us to rest.

It rouses the heart to gladness,
   Like music's nameless power;
It thrills the heart with sadness,
   The solemn evening hour.

TO DIAMOND, A PET CANARY.

Little songster, though a captive,
   Still thy happy voice is heard,
Through the live long summer day,—
   Thou sing'st merrily, sweet bird.

Thou art no puling mourner,
   Because thou art not free.;
Thy voice rings out as merrily
   As on the forest tree.

Sweet little joyous friend,
   I hear each pleasant note,
As if it was a grateful prayer,
   Welling from thy tiny throat.

And thou teachest me a lesson,
   From the music of thy voice—
Ever to thank kind heaven,
   And prayerfully rejoice.

KIND WORDS.

Kind words soothe and gently cheer,
Are to the sorrowing doubly dear;
They wield a high and mighty power,
Felt in every scene, in every hour.
They soothe every woe, quell every grief,
And to the blighted bring relief;
They throw a spell of magic rare
Upon the soul struck with despair.

Kind words, they dry the childish tear,
That springs from the eyes of children dear;
Welcome they fall on the bursting heart
Of the soldier, who is compelled to part

KIND WORDS.

From the friends of his youth, and go afar,
Encountering the storms and chance of war:
Those last kind words he treasures deep,
Their sweet remembrance he does keep.

Kind words still the suffering breast
Of those who cannot find a rest;
Their life is crushed with fearful pain,
They feel as if even hope was vain.
They weep and wail, they are so lone,
For all they truly loved are gone,—
But the deep spell of kind, kind words,
Have cheered and thrilled their bosoms' chords.

'Tis sweet to hear a holy hymn,
Sung when the sultry day grows dim;
Sweet to see the evening star
Shining on the hills afar,—

KIND WORDS.

Sweet to see the glowing flowers,
Cheering the smiling summer hours,—
But sweeter far, above them all,
Are kind, kind words that gently fall.

Joyous to hear the hunter's horn,
On a laughing rosy morn,—
Joyous to hear the blackbird's note,
When he sings in a fairy grot,—
Joyous to hear a stirring lay,
Sung when the heart is brightly gay,—
But more joyous still it is to hear
Kind words from those we love so dear.

ON A FAVOURITE DOG.

Faithful friend, thou sitt'st beside me,
    Thine eyes are bent on mine,—
Lovingly they gaze upon me,
    And truthfully they shine.
Perusing carefully my face,
    As if thou fain wouldst know,
As if thou fain could find no trace,
    Of sadness on my brow.

When thou seest nought but smiles,
    And I, no longer sad;
Thou then displays a thousand wiles,
    To shew that thou art glad.

ON A FAVOURITE DOG.

Thy fearless, true, and honest look,
  Tells thou art no ingrate;
All may read thee like a book,
  Thou art no deceiving hypocrite.

Mute faithful friend, thy love is pure,
  Praise thou dost deserve;
Thy friendship is unstained and sure,
  No bribe could make thee swerve.
I wish that all the friends I meet,
  Were something more like thee;
Life's cup would share a draught most sweet,
  If all were staunch to me.

THOU SHALT BE LOVED BY ME.

When I am alone, and musing,
   Other years fly back to me;
The blithsome, happy days of yore,
   'Tis then I think of thee.

When the moon's pale light is falling
   On the blooming hawthorn tree;
Under its branches oft we sported,
   'Tis then I think of thee.

When I walk on a surf beat shore,
   And listen to a moaning sea;
It calls forth a soft remembrance,
   And then I think of thee.

To forget my dearest friend,
   Ah; that can never be;
For while life and memory lasts,
   Thou shall be loved by me.

THE PRAIRIE, OR THE FAR WEST.

The mountains rise in mighty grandeur,
    Where feet of men have seldom trod;
Fresh as the morning of creation,
    Wearing the impress of their God.
The blue circle of the heavens girding
    Round about the open plain,
Where the turf with brilliant greenness,
    Never human foot did stain.

Here the Monarda, sweetly shedding
    Perfume from its purple flowers;
There the Malva, proudly rearing
    Its clustering scarlet towers.

And the fragrant, bright Ascelpia,
  Is redolent with bloom;
The eye never tires in gazing
  On the blossoms of the Cleome.

The air is filled with delicious odour,
  Flowery insects flap their wing;
Wild bees drink a honeyed nectar,
  As among the buds they cling.
Then again the scene it changes,
  And it is the forest deep;
Massive limbs of huge trees stretching,
  Like a giant in his sleep.

Graceful antelopes are grazing,
  Without one pang of fear;
Droves of buffalo on the vistas,
  And herds of lordly deer.

THE PRAIRIE.

Many groves with clumps of copsewood,
    Colossal cedars waving free ;
Fairy white moss festoons the branches,
    Hanging like drapery from the tree.

Music fills the air with sweetness,
    The paroquet, and redbird singing,
The pecker, and the cicada,
    Together all are ringing.
The eye wanders forth delighted,
    Down the flashing sunlit glade ;
And the woods are warm and glorious,
    In the beechen forest shade.

They to whom a mind is given,
    And who those plains explore ;
They may have a faint imagining,
    Of that far viewless shore.

When gazing on these woods primeval,
 Where so few have ever trod;
They must bow before the presence,
 The might, and majesty of God.

SEPTEMBER.

The Autumn leaves are falling fast,
They tell us summer days are past;
But the reaper binds the golden wheat,
And that is a sight most fair to greet.
The dew drops glisten in the morning ray,
Like diamonds decking it bright and gay:
The village bells ring a merry chime,
As if laughing at old father time.
The ploughman whistles in the new mown dale,
And the sheep are bleating in the vale;
The breezy wind so fresh and free,
Whirls with a gleeful melody.
The woods are flushed with a glorious dye,
Teeming with mirth and radiant joy;
Peace, beauty, and love abound,
Shedding a gladness all around.
The sun sinks brightly to his rest,
Lighting with glory the glowing west;
For it is the month of joy and health,
And earth yields her stores of wealth.

TO A BEAUTIFUL SLEEPING CHILD.

There thou liest fat and rosy,
In thy warm cot so cosy,—
Thy chubby hands are soft and sleek,
Mischief lies in thy dimpled cheek.
Thy sunny face is lit with smiles,
As if dreaming of thy coming wiles;
On thy fair head, bright curls are flowing,
Like zephyrs in the west wind blowing.
Thou art a picture lying there,
Thy pretty limbs, they are so fair,—
Every attitude of thine is grace,
Beauty shines on thy lovely face.
Thy motions are so free and wild,
Charming, gleesome, winning child;
Thou art a very cupid in thyself,
Thou blithsome, happy little elf.

VERSES TO A LADY.

The violet flower, modest and sweet,
    And the lovely primrose pale,—
And that type of all things pure,
    The white lily of the vale.

Pure as those flowers thou art,
    They all resemble thee;
May thy bloom be unlike theirs,—
    Never blighted may it be.

May thy smiles of radiant joy,
    Thy soft and glancing eye,
Thy graceful sylph-like form,
    With soft tones breathing melody,

Never know an hour of sorrow,
  Never over treachery weep,
But may every blessed spirit,
  Always guard thy holy sleep.

May thy good heart ever feel,
  For another's piercing woe ;
And gently soothe the stricken soul,
  By heavy grief laid low.

To those who need thy succour
  Lend a willing helping hand ;
So thou shalt be blessed for ever,
  Thy heart with love expand.

On thy path a sovereign power,
  A glory round shall spread ;
Shall on that day when He rewards,
  Place heaven's crown on thy head.

HEALTH.

What are the hoarded coffers of wealth,
Compared to that best of blessings, health;
Men may possess great stores of gold,
And princely gems of price untold,—
They may own broad acres of sunny land,
And high in the esteem of all may stand—
But the lowest peasant that tills their ground,
With a healthy frame, strong and sound,
Is richer than they with all their wealth,
He possesses the priceless gift of health.
When the heavy eye is dimmed with pain,
Then the choicest gifts of earth are vain;
They cannot give strength to the sinking voice,
Or bid the poor sick heart rejoice,—
When jaded and sad on the weary bed,
And sleep cannot visit the tortured head;
Ah! then how poor are heaps of wealth,
Compared to the rich treasure of health.

ON A BUNCH OF WITHERED FLOWERS.

That bunch of lovely flowers,
   So blooming yesterday;
Already they are drooping,
   And fading fast to-day.

The blushing mossy rose,
   So grateful to the sight;
Alas! her bloom is gone,
   That shone so soft and bright.

The modest daisy white,
   That lay snugly in its bed,
By the side of the crystal stream,
   Its beauty is now dead.

ON A BUNCH OF WITHERED FLOWERS.

And the dazzling tinted tulip,
   Hangs low its lofty head;
And the pretty primrose pale,
   That fragrance sweetly shed.

They that shone so proudly,
   In the garden gay,
Are robbed of all their graces,
   And withering fast away.

All things here are fleeting,
   Aye, fleeting as those flowers;
Let us then improve in goodness,
   The quickly flying hours.

ON VIEWING A RUINED CASTLE BY MOONLIGHT.

I mused upon that hoary ruin,
    That mouldering pile decayed,—
I see the black and crumbling arches,
    By the pale moon's flickering shade.
Through the dark decaying aisles,
    The wind does strangely howl;
And nought is heard around,
    But the screech of the grey-eyed owl.

For the glory of other years,
    Is fast turning into dust,—
Those rich and lofty towers,
    Are succumbing to time's rust.

THE RUINED CASTLE.

They now are all laid waste,
    Those gorgeous princely halls;
Gaunt ruin is staring bare,
    And only falling walls.

But the deep and rolling river,
    Is unchanged as on that day
When that castle rose in grandeur,
    It still winds its silvery way.
It flows the same as in other years,
    When that structure in its glory,
Was the home of the fair and brave,—
    The renowned of ancient story.

The river is a type of God,
    And emblem of His might;
While that work of human hands,
    Decays before His sight.

WATER.

The following is the inscription on a Turkish street Fountain:—

"Rest, O traveller! for this is the fountain of enjoyment; rest here, as under the shadow of the Plane-tree, for this roof casts a shade as deep as that of the Cypress, but with more of joy. Ask one day of the angels in Eden, if this water is not as delicious as the rivers of that garden, or as the stream of Zemzem Sultan Achmet, the second Alexander,—he whose glory is as the sun, and his generosity perpetually increasing like the tree of life, has reared this Kiosk, and stamped it with his signet ring. This water flows unceasingly, like his benevolence, as well for the king as the beggar, the wise man and the fool. The first of all the blessings of Allah is water."

It is the last sentence of this Inscription, that suggested the following lines. It is only in the burning climes of the East, that the inestimable blessing of water is known and appreciated, and recognised as it ought to be, as one of the first of the blessings of God. No wonder, then, that a people so rich in flowery language, and feeling the value of water, should inscribe such eloquent inscriptions on the fountains in their streets.

In the fiery East, on the arid sultry plain,
The traveller sighs for water, but sighs in vain,
Not a blade of grass relieves his weary eye,
He feels all strength and energy within him die,

The humblest plant cannot even there be found,—
Nothing but scorching sand or flinty ground;
No Jessamine bowers, with their rich perfume,
Nor Olive trees with their fragrant bloom,—
No gushing fountains whose waters he may lave,
No silvery stream with its crystal wave,—
Only the burning sun and glistening sand;
For it is the dry trackless desert land.
He thinks with agony of his distant home,
Of his native mountains where he did roam,
Of the bracing breeze of his country's hills,
Its murmuring streams, and gurgling rills,—
Fainting and drooping he still wanders on,
But his cheek is pale, hope is almost gone.

Ah! hailing his straining sight at last,
An oasis in the distant sandy waste,
Sweet hope imparts a soothing strength,
And he reaches that haven of life at length,
'Neath creeping plants, a streamlet hidden lay,
As sweet, as cool, and pure as cloudless day.

WATER.

No sight was ever to him so fair,
As that little stream in the desert there.
Eagerly his scorching lips he did lave,
And cooled his hand in its rippling wave ;
Rich draught it was to his burning breath,
For his soul was thirsting nigh to death.
New strength was given to his weary feet,
By that crystal like water, soft and sweet ;
His heart did thrill, with a grateful joy,
All things looked well to his raptured eye.
Through the desert he did onward press,
With high glowing hopes of happiness ;
The talisman that made his path so sure,
Was the priceless water true and pure.

Water ! water ! is nature's constant cry,
Without it who can breathe, they die,—
The little birds that sing on every tree.
And roam the wild wood flying free,—
The lowing cattle in the dewy vale,
And the bleating sheep in the grassy dale,—

The flowers that flourish rich and gay,
And spread in beauty round many a way,—
The lofty trees, with branches waving wide,
That line the forest on every side,—
The rich and heavy ripening grain,
That waves with high head on the fertile plain,—
The sun is looking on them with fiery breath,
And they all are dry and thirsting to death;
Water! water! is their earnest cry,—
Give us water or else we die.

Water! 'tis to man a boon that's given,
By the mercy of the bounteous king of heaven;
One of the greatest gifts He did bestow,
On his creatures for their comfort here below.
It cools the wrought and over-heated brain,
When every other remedy has proved in vain;
Pours high health into the sluggish veins of life,
And fraught with every blessing it is rife.
Many are the diseases it has soothed and cured,—
Without it pain could not have been endured;

WATER.

It is the draught, that does the greatest good,
And yet the drink that is least understood.
No human soul could live, and want it long,
The very essences of life to it belong;
It is the draught the Almighty Himself gave
To man to strengthen him, and to save.
Well has the oriental spoken, when he said,
It is the first of blessings God has shed
Upon mankind; high in rank or small,
He gives the priceless gift alike to all:
Let all prize it, drink it cool and pure,
The soul to crime, it never will allure.
Then may water! water! be the eager cry,
Of they who by strong drink daily death do die.

TRUE HAPPINESS.

Where is true happiness to be found?
  That great and priceless treasure,
Is it in the chambers of the great,
  Or in the haunts of pleasure?

Is it to be found in the bacchant's cup,
  Filled with the ruby wine?
Or in the dazzling merry dance,
  Where beauty fair doth shine?

Is it to be found on the gilded shrine,
  Where the votaries of fashion bow?
Where the lips are wreathed in smiles,
  And splendour there doth glow.

TRUE HAPPINESS.

Is it to be found in the palace halls,
  Where luxury round is spread?
And every rare and costly jewel,
  Decks the regal crowned head.

Is it to be found in the warrior's deeds,
  When the air with shouts resounds?
When a nation's love pours forth,
  And the conqueror's brow is crowned.

Is it to be found on the battle plain,
  When the hero his life doth yield?
But not till he hears the joyous cry,
  That he was his country's shield.

Is it to be found on the deathless page,
  That reveals the poet's feeling?
Soothing many a silent hour,
  O'er the heart with sweetness stealing.

TRUE HAPPINESS.

In the visions that fancy weaves,
    Can it there be truly found?
Or in the magic spell of words,
    Or the spirit rapture bound.

Is it to be found in glorious scenes,
    Of mountain, hills, or streams?
Or in the works of worth and art,
    Or high heroic themes.

Among the gifted sons of song,
    Has it there its dwelling?
When the ear drinks in the silver strains,
    And every thought is telling.

Is it to be found in the noble ship,
    Breasting the boundless sea?
Where the waves are dancing high,
    And the soul is swelling free.

TRUE HAPPINESS.

Is it to be found near the despot king,
 With millions at his command?
Who rules with unflinching power,
 A devoted slavish land.

Ah, no! its home is not with these,
 It cares not for rank or fame,—
It seeks far other scenes of life,
 Heeds no high sounding name.

In the home of the noble man,
 Who midst the cares of life,
Finds yet sufficient time
 To soothe another's strife.

Who when the heart is blighted,
 And the haughty spirit laid low,
O'er that faulty but repentant soul,
 Does loving kindness shew.

TRUE HAPPINESS.

To the grieved or mourning heart,
    Has a holy word or prayer;
And ever acts most kindly,
    To the bosom fraught with care.

Who when friends are in distress,
    Puts forth his willing hand;
Though their wealth has flown away,
    Does by them firmly stand.

When danger is near the youthful mind,
    He never does them forsake;
Tries by intreaty and kind deeds,
    Their conscience to awake.

There in the home of such a man,
    True happiness makes its stay;
And true glory crowns his brow,
    Deep blessings line his way.

TRUE HAPPINESS.

'Tis only in the path of duty
We find happiness at the goal;
There our striving will be crowned—
Heaven's sunshine gild the soul.

A TRAVELLER VIEWING THE GREAT PRAIRIE FOR THE FIRST TIME.

In the regions of the far west, watered by the great Missouri,
Dwell the Indian tribes of the Sioux, the Deleware, and the Pawnee;
There roams the wild horse, the buffalo and the lordly deer,
Free as the mighty wind and knowing no pang of fear.
The traveller rode onward, day after day, night after night,
In the midst of great forests, till at last on his eager sight
Burst the great and boundless Prairie, like a swelling sea;
A vast ocean of grass, limitless, wild and free.

The sun rose in floods of glory, blazing on the
    scene,
Grassy islands, giant trees, covered with his
    golden sheen ;
Brilliant glades of forest green, and belts of
    flowery land ;
Thickets of shrubbery, there nature shone sub-
    lime and grand,—
Myriads of the rarest flowers were gemming the
    way,—
Thousands of gorgeous birds, singing to the
    sunny day,—
Cerulean was the sky, and untrammelled swept
    the soft breeze,
Among the groups of islands, and clumps of
    the willow trees,—
Herds of bison, in their glory were careering
    o'er the plain,
The wild ass and graceful antelope, following
    the exciting train.

He gazed upon the wondrous scene, and his
    heart was swelling,
Mighty was the language that primeval plain
    was telling;
Solemn grandeur reigned around—words they
    could not tell,
The worship to the Infinite, which did his bosom
    swell,—
The blood gushed wildly through his veins, his
    forehead hot was flushing,
His eyes flashed, glorious thoughts through his
    heart was rushing,—
Speechless with emotion, his throbbing heart it
    quickly gasped*—
The reins fell on his horse's neck, his nervous
    hands he clasped,—
Sigh after sigh burst from out his panting heav-
    ing chest,

   * This incident is recorded by one of our most talented
writers on Prairie Life.

At length a smothered Oh! came from his
    surcharged breast;
The Prairie he had pictured, when roaming by
    his native streams,—
He had fancied it in various forms in his youth-
    ful dreams,—
But a vision such as this his finest thoughts did
    ne'er command,
As that grand primeval plain planned by an
    Almighty hand.
He seized the reins, with one mad plunge he
    bounded on that plain,—
To have stopped him in that fearful race it
    would have been in vain.
Untrammeled freedom, he never knew, nor felt
    it until now,
And his whole heart and mind, and thought did
    before his Maker bow.
In after years fair sights he saw, but never one
    like that again,
Nor e'er forgot that glorious ride on the great
    Prairie plain.

VERSES TO * * * *

In every phase of life I found thee good and true,
The world to me would dreary be if not for you;
Thy heart for me did ever right and nobly feel,
Thou hast cheered me on through woe and weal.
When sorrow blenched my cheek with many a tear,
Thou soothed and vanquished every boding fear;
Blest and happy I have ever been with thee,
For kind and watchful hast thou been of me.
Well hast thou laboured to ward off grief or pain,

And bring back happy hours of hope again;
Thy love has lighted up life's fitful dream,
Making all things bright and cheerful seem.
Thy good deeds in my heart shall treasured be,
Ever shall they dwell on the shrine of memory;
May God in goodness pour blessings on thy head,
And many rich gifts round thy path be shed.

THOUGHTS ON THE DEATH OF A TYRANT.

He whose hand in cruel vengeance,
    Oppressed the weary soul;
Whose unshrinking haughty pride,
    Spurned and defied control.

He whose dread command,
    Doomed the brave a fearful fate;
Who poured out blood like water,
    In his revengeful hate.

Who deemed himself scarce mortal,
    Triumphant in his sway;
What is he now? the despot,—
    A piece of senseless clay.

THOUGHTS ON THE DEATH OF A TYRANT.

A mighty hand has struck him down,
In the height of strife;
In midst of mocking grandeur,
Cut off his days of life.

Yes! he who made the noble
Groan beneath his iron rod;
Stands to give his dread account,
Before an angry God.

THE END.

GENERAL BEM AND OTHER POEMS.
BY MRS L. A. CZARNECKI.

Second Edition enlarged. Edinburgh: A. Fullarton & Co.
Price 2s. 6d.

Opinions of the Press.

THE authoress of this neat little volume of Poetry, although bearing a Polish surname, is, we understand, a Scottish lady; and we may mention the fact for the reader's information, as the subjects of many of the pieces, coupled with the name, had almost deluded us into the belief that Mrs Czarnecki was a native Sarmatian. That she is a Polish patriot there can be no doubt, as in addition to the "Lines on General Bem," we find poems entitled "The Dying Captive in Siberia," "The Polish Mother, or the Fate of a Polish Household," and "Poland and the Poles in the late Hungarian Struggle for Liberty," all breathing a warm and glowing sympathy in the cause of that interesting but down-trodden land. But while this is the characteristic of a number of the pieces, the strain of the most of them is of a domestic and religious kind, which cannot fail to recommend the volume to numerous readers.—*North British Daily Mail.*

This work is the production of a Scottish lady, now the wife of a distinguished exile in this country. Though there is the indication of a Scottish mind in this little volume, it has an additional charm from the earnestness with which the authoress enters into the circumstances of Hungary, and the deep sympathy she evidently feels with its noble though downcast children. The volume is made up of miscellaneous pieces, some of them of a religious character, such as "The Peace of the Sabbath," "Before the Throne in Prayer," "Where can the Heart have Peace?"—*Glasgow Examiner.*

Mrs Czarnecki's pretty little volume contains some praiseworthy verses. It is pervaded by the love of liberty, the sense of moral beauty, and a pious sympathy with the doctrines of the gospel.—*Scottish Guardian.*

A well-intentioned little volume, breathing a spirit of freedom and piety.—*Glasgow Citizen.*

Mrs Czarnecki, the writer of the volume before us, we can hardly be wrong in concluding is a native of our own island, acquainted with our customs and manners, and familiar with the idioms of our language. She has dedicated

OPINIONS OF THE PRESS.

her little work to one of our distinguished citizens, William Campbell, Esq., of Tillichewan. The piece which she has devoted to General Bem occupies only three pages of the volume, but even that rendered it quite appropriate to place a name so distinguished at the head of the volume. The pieces are in all thirty-three, in which trodden-down Poland and Hungary, as might have been expected, come in for a share of the writer's poetic musings. There are several pieces of a religious nature, and all have a good moral tendency. "Jochonan, or the City of the Demons," is a terrible story, but it has a good moral.—*Christian News.*

This handsome volume of poetry is the production of a Scottish lady, who is now the wife of a Polish exile in this country. As may be inferred from the title, Hungary and Poland—their wrongs, and their heroic efforts to redress them—occupy a large portion of its pages; while the remainder are devoted to miscellaneous pieces of moral and religious tendency. The style is easy and smooth; and the entire work breathes an earnestness and patriotism, which cannot fail to be captivating and elevating. We have no hesitation in recommending this elegant little volume to the attention of the lovers of poetry.—*Stirling Observer.*

This volume is by a Scottish lady, the wife of a resident Pole, and as their title may indicate, they are strongly patriotic towards the Polish and Hungarian cause. The majority of the pieces are moreover written with considerable taste and feeling, and do much credit to the lady's heart as well as head. The most ambitious piece in the volume is Jochonan, or the City of the Demons, which displays considerable merit.—*Glasgow Sentinel.*

"General Bem and Other Poems." A volume under this title has just been published by Mrs Czarnecki. The lady is a native of Scotland, but is married to a Pole, and her writings exhibit a warm sympathy for the unfortunate country of her husband.—*Carlisle Journal.*

This is a neat little volume of verse, handsomely printed and bound, and dedicated to William Campbell, Esq. of Tillichewan Castle, as a tribute of admiration to that public and private character which has secured for him universal esteem. The contents are various, and some of the poems have already appeared in the newspapers. The fair authoress, a Scotchwoman, we believe, is warmly attached to the Hungarian cause, and employs her pen in recording the praises of its great chiefs.—*Glasgow Constitutional.*

"General Bem and other Poems." A pretty little volume under this title has been published. It is the production of Mrs L. A. Czarnecki, a Scotchwoman, notwithstanding the Polish patronymic she derives from her husband, and the warm sympathy she shows with Polish and Hungarian wrongs. Many of her pieces are smoothly and pleasantly written, and their tendency as a whole is patriotic, pure, and devout.—*Glasgow Chronicle.*

We beg to direct the special attention of the public generally to the Advertisement of Mrs Czarnecki. Our contemporaries in every district in Scotland have eulogised her style and taste as exhibited in General Bem and other poems, and all that remains for us to say, is simply, that they breathe a glowing fervour of Christian feeling, and display great ability.—*Campbelton Journal.*

OPINIONS OF THE PRESS.

This is a pretty little volume of poetry, the production of a Scotch lady, the Polish patronymic the authoress derives from her husband, and her verses are smoothly and pleasantly written, and breathe a genuine spirit of piety, patriotism, and a love of liberty.—*Gromock Herald*

"General Bem and other Poems." The poetry breathes both a patriotic and Christian spirit, and the reviews which have appeared in several of our contemporaries speak very highly of it.—*Ayr Advertiser*.

Extract of Letter from the Right Honourable the Earl of Carlisle.

"General Bem and other Poems." The volume seems filled with good and graceful poetry.—Lord Carlisle.

Extract of Letter from the late Count Valerian Krasinski, Author of "Panslavism and Germanism," "History of the Reformation in Poland," "Sketches of the Religious History of the Slavonic Nations."

I have read "General Bem and other Poems" with feelings of the greatest pleasure. The lines are full of patriotic sentiment, and at the same time breathe a spirit of earnestness and true Christian thought, pervaded by pure and graceful language.—Your sincere friend, Valerian Krasinski.

Extract of Letter from Captain Rzczynski, (Knight of the Golden Cross Virtuti Militari) Author of "The Valley of Death, or the Famous Charge of the British Light Cavalry at the Battle of Balaklava," etc. etc.

Hearing it related that you are going to publish a new volume of poetry, in which enterprise I wish you much prosperity and success. Judging from the earnestness with which you entered into the circumstances of Poland and Hungary, in your immortal "Lines on General Bem," with whom I was personally acquainted, and fought the Russians in the glorious battles of Gruchow and Ostrolenka, etc., and many more, and for the same cause, and the deep interest you evidently take, and the warm sympathy you seem to feel, makes me confident that the forthcoming poems will be perradod with the same patriotic and choice religious feeling and good moral tendency with which your poems so gloriously shine, and which I have read with much interest and true satisfaction.—I have the honour, Dear Madam, to be your obedient Servant, Rzczynski.

OPINIONS OF THE PRESS.

THE ROTHESAY WALTZES, AND BUTE POLKA, for the Pianoforte. By Mrs L. A. Czarnecki. Second Edition, price 2s. 6d. Wood & Co., Edinburgh and Glasgow.

THE TREMBOULA WALTZES, for the Pianoforte. By Mrs L. A. Czarnecki. Seventh Edition, price 3s. London: Addison & Co., 210 Regent Street.

THE RAGLAN QUADRILLES, for the Pianoforte. By Mrs L. A. Czarnecki. Second Edition, price 3s. Edinburgh: Patterson & Son, George Street. London: Chappel, 50 New Bond Street.

The Raglan Quadrilles are, as their name imparts, intended to embody some of the martial spirit of the present day, in the light and agreeable form of dance music, and to a certain extent, the composer has succeeded in producing an effect not always found as a characteristic of such emanations.—*The Dublin Daily Express.*

The "Raglan Quadrilles," is the title given by Madam L. A. Czarnecki, the talented composer, to five spirited and charming Quadrilles which she has composed, and which have just been published. Madam Czarnecki is a Scotch lady, who has already acquired a reputation for musical composition, the "Tremboula Waltzes," the "Rothesay Waltzes," and the "Bute Polka," being the fruits of her pen, and all of them affording undoubted proof of their authoress being a lady of exquisite musical taste and skill. We are, therefore, not surprised to find, that she has met with flattering encomiums from the Northern Press, and we imagine that those talents which have caused her productions to stand in high reputation amongst musical circles "over the border," will place her in equally enviable position in the estimation of her more Southern countrymen and women.—*The Durham Chronicle.*

The "Raglan Quadrilles," are light, gay, spirited, and sparkling,—they are pleasing additions to the music of the boudoir and saloon.—*Belfast Chronicle.*

The "Tremboula Waltzes,"—This is the title of a set of Waltzes composed and dedicated to the Lord Advocate, by Mrs L. A. Czarnecki, already known by compositions of a similar character. The "Tremboula Waltzes" are three in number, of a very plain and simple description, and one at least of them—the third—possesses claims to the notice of those who purchase this class of music, far beyond some other productions which we could name.—*Scotsman.*

We are happy in being able to recommend to the attention of our fair readers, the "Tremboula Waltzes," by a Scotch Lady, the "Tremboula

OPINIONS OF THE PRESS.

Waltzes," three in number, are very pretty, and in their structure exceedingly simple. We have had the pleasure of hearing them played, and consider the third of them especially beautiful in a high degree. The position of the Authoress Madam Czarnecki, is sufficiently determined by the fact, that these Waltzes are by permission dedicated to the Lord Advocate.—*Stirling Observer.*

The "Tremboula Waltzes,"—A series of Waltzes has just been published under the above name, .The Authoress is Mrs L. A. Czarnecki, a Scotch lady, who has already given some other musical compositions to the world. The "Tremboula Waltzes" are very fair specimens of this class of music, and evidence the possession by the Authoress of excellent musical taste. We have no doubt they will become popular, and we bespeak for them a large sale.—*Stirling Advertiser.*

The "Tremboula Waltzes,"—The lady whose compositions are named above, has rendered herself favourably known to the musical public, by similar efforts of a like nature. The Waltzes are characterised by much good taste, and simplicity of arrangements, and they well deserve, as we are certain they will obtain, an extensive degree of patronage. The Authoress is an admirable pianist.—*Inverness Advertiser.*

The "Tremboula Waltzes' display much simplicity, and beauty as compositions, and their whole arrangement is very creditable to the musical taste of the fair Authoress, they are besides, the production of a Scotch lady, and not her first effort either in a style of composition for which her talents seem well adapted ; and these circumstances independent of their merits, must, we think, secure for them a cordial reception by the Waltz admiring portion of our countrymen.—*Aberdeen Journal.*

Beautiful compositions are these same "Tremboula Waltzes." We are not surprised to find Madam Czarnecki's Waltzes in such favour with the ladies. Very recently we had the good fortune to hear them played by a distinguished pianist. Remarkable alike for their simplicity and beauty as compositions, we can safely say, that more delightful pieces of their kind, we never remember to have listened to. The Waltzes afford most undoubted proof of their authoress being a lady of exquisite musical taste and skill. —*Arbroath Guide.*

The "Tremboula Waltzes" are marked by a pleasing simplicity and beauty of style, and do manifest considerable taste in the composer. The "Rothsay Waltzes" and the "Bute Polka" by the same Authoress, already possess some repute in musical circles, having reached a second edition.—*Newcastle Courant.*

www.ingramcontent.com/pod-product-compliance
Lightning Source LLC
Chambersburg PA
CBHW030401170426
43202CB00010B/1448